# The Struggle to Find True Love

by Holly Flame Maxey

CITI OF
BOOKS

# The Struggle to

# Find True Love

**CITIOFBOOKS, INC.**
3736 Eubank NE Suite A1
Albuquerque, NM 87111-3579
*www.citiofbooks.com*

Hotline: 1 (877) 389-2759
Fax: 1 (505) 930-7244

Ordering Information:
Quantity sales. Special discounts are available on quantity purchases by corporations, associations, and others. For details, contact the publisher at the address above.

Printed in the United States of America.

| ISBN-13: | Softcover | 978-1-959682-12-7 |
|---|---|---|
| | Hardcover | 978-1-959682-14-1 |
| | eBook | 978-1-959682-13-4 |

Library of Congress Control Number:    2022919448

# Contents

# Remember.....Life is a Journey

There is a man who possess my mind,
my heart, and my soul.
Or should I say
There is a man who free's my mind,
my heart and my soul
He did it in an unconventional way
Nonetheless he did it

The sensations of a mid-spring day
Come to mind
The fresh air slowly cooling down
My desires to always be on the move

Every day I feel calmer
Every day I feel at peace
Knowing that God will never leave me
God will never leave us

Life is a journey, not a race
We all need to participate
We all need to slow down
And realize the only way to win the race
Is not to run

# My love, you consume my every breath

I offer you my complete devotion
My heart, mind, and soul honor your aura
I am entranced by the entrance way to your soul
My life is enriched when I think about all the ways
You shine and bring light to my life

My days pass by effortlessly
Inspiration comes to me in dewdrops
Of love
These innate desires require no response
They exist naturally, only to dance with the butterflies
That have taken residency
in the deepest parts of my existence

Thinking about you my love
Is no longer an option, it is my very breath
 My complete knowledge of existence
How can I live without breathing?
How can I breathe without the knowledge of
The awesome existential "you"

# Thinking about what you said

You should not think that you are annoying
Because...
You are....you are annoying
And that is ok...really it is ok
Acceptance is key in moving on
When you can accept who you are
You can arrange your life
Accordingly
Say to yourself
I am a poet and I am annoying
And that is ok
You will never have a personal relationship
 But do not despair
Knowledge is emancipation
There is freedom in emancipation
Most importantly remember
Whatever is annoying to someone else
Is fun for you
And the only person who will never leave you
is you?

# A prayer from my heart

If there is ever a doubt in your mind
How much I love you, just look up to the sky
And remember that I tell the moon every night
And the light you see from the moon
Is really from my heart

In my dreams we dance together
In my dreams I am whole, I am who you desire
Our journey together is my only destination

The ability to dream, to hope for better
Yet, to be happy where I am right now
Frustration never killed anyone
Fear and love cannot occupy the same house
Trust, Belief, and Love
Are the only way to be delivered
From the pain

I reluctantly say to you my beloved
That at this time I am lost
Lost in the delusions of my mind
Trapped in the pain of psychological time

Find me, Free me
and I will be forever yours
and you will be forever mine
This is my true prayer every day/every night

# Don't ask what you do not want to know

Questions revel truth that should be left unknown

Fear runs in circles. death is certain

Life is not

A search for the light. turns into a fight for life

What is life? What is the truth?

How can we appreciate life without

Feeling the hot breath of darkness

Constantly on our backs

Keeping us down

Who made us and put us here

Can free our hearts, our minds

Yet;; where do we search?

Where do we find this being or beings

Why search; when they have always been inside?

We should focus on our commonalities

Instead of our differences

Life is fast in perspective

Looking back, we can be more objective

Looking forward we think more of death

Try to find what was always there I look and I look

And I find is tears, pain & destruction
Death is priceless, Just as life
You cannot have one without the other
Free me, Kill my heart
I desire nothing in life
I only want peace in death

# My Beloved

You are my first thought as I rise
my last thought as my soul escapes my body at night
you are my every breath in between
My heart refuses to beat without thoughts of you

Our communication is sacred
I count the hours until our souls
get the chance to reconnect

When i feel you inside me
I can feel the life good
I can feel myself as good
waking up every morning
seeing life through your eyes
is nothing short of amazing

Time is nonexistent yet simultaneously endless
when your essence is away
I pray one day that the gap between us
disappears forever

I pray one day that all our vibrations
become manifested reality
of all we intended them to be

# Can you see me?

Before she came into my life
no one saw me
no one knew who i was or even cared to know
but now that has all changed

with the appearance of my personal angel
the love of my life
my soul, my heart
my reason for waking every morning

you can see who I am beyond
what she tells everyone
you can see me for who I am
not for who everyone needs me to be

They need me to be safe
They need me to be controlled
I can tell when I look into your eyes
you like my edge, you like my fire

Just come a little closer and
I will take you higher

# Inner Conflict

I do not like you right now
I love you. I need you
I just do not like you
you make my soul, my heart, my mind
work so hard
For my own emancipation

I literally feel like
I am being driven by my passions
That will put me on my pathway to success
But I will arrive there alone

Alone, Alone
Forever and always alone
I suffer, I cry this endless, enduring pain
But you do not care
You cannot see the pain I will feel

When you eventually leave. and I know this because
eventually everyone does
I will end up drowning
In my unanswered pool of desires

It is inevitable that I will end up alone
Only with my thoughts, my unanswered burning desires

My illusive rainbow of dreams
Alone with my demons that tell me that I am
Unlovable, untouchable

So, while you are still here
Speak to me just one word of encouragement
That i can hang onto
That will be my one thread of hope
To carry me onto the day of my death
Where I will undeniably end up alone

# Is it a probability?

How long has it been since
I have last seen you
My beloved
My heart
My reason for breathing

Has it been a week
A year
No...it has only been 12 hours
I want to email you but...
I am afraid you will think I am too clingy
I am afraid you might think me
As undesirable

God knows I think of you
With my every breath
I am in so much pain
In this moment
I do not know how i will survive
The next 156 hours without
even
being able to email you

My words being read by you

Bring me hope
My thoughts in your mind
Bring me peace

I pray every day
For this torture to end
I pray every day
For you, For me
For Us
If it is possible for there ever
To be an US

# Your soul knows my name

Faster, Harder, Deeper
into my heart your journey begins
What is your final destination ?
My beloved

Wherever you go; I will go with you
Whatever you do; I will do with you
Your eyes own my soul
your breath knows my every desire

Everyday is completely exhilarating
When I can look at the enchanting
Portal to your soul
Take me with you anywhere
Take me anywhere, anytime

Only your embrace can
Keep my fire hot and peaceful simultaneously
Only your embrace can ease
The suffering tension that I feel
When your presence is absent

# Please tell me.....I am not annoying

It has been brought to my attention
That if I do not try…
I already lost
So, here i am
Even though i am hiding behind my words
I am still here

Admitting to you behind my tears
That my heart refuses to beat
Without any communication with you
Why won't you let me email you
How can I ease this pain

I am drowning in my tears
I pray for any kind of relief
But It never comes
I am afraid of rejection
Yet I never even given you the chance
To reject me

So, in the final seconds of the clock
I am admitting to you
And everyone else who reads this
I love you and miss you

Every day I do not properly
Express my emotions to you

Please end my suffering
By at least saying
I am not annoying to you

# Never ever have I

I have traveled and experienced
Six different countries/cultures
Explored 48 continental united states
Yet, I have never encountered
A soul such as yours before
And I doubt that I ever will

I will tell you this once
That if I would have found anyone
Remotely like you; I would be there
And not here right now
I would not be thinking about you 168/7
(There is 168 hours in a week)

You possess something
No one in the world ever has or ever will
My heart, my mind, my spirit
Apart from your acquisition of these Y
ou make them better
Then you return them to me

I admire how effortlessly
You mold me into a better person
How my perspective of life

Is enhanced
I pray that our paths never part
That we can be united in every way
And never have to feel the pain
Of separation

# I am awake

I am trying to understand
Either you do not remember or...you just forgot?
You were the one who woke me.....
I am not enlightened, but I am awake
What now? What are your plans for me
My beloved

I like feeling you deep inside me
The deeper you go the softer and wetter I become
Until I drown in the warmth of your soul
And I can feel eternity calling our names

If i can not be with you; my love
I might as well be a millionaire
Money always comes second to Love
Money does not bring happiness
Only a distraction until death overtakes me
I wish it was you that would overtake me instead
Arouse my desires
Follow the path least taken
And It will lead us both home

# No evidence?

How can I tell you that I love you
When I do not even believe that it exists
I am a writer, a poet and a dreamer
Or I was before.
Reality overtook my brain

I can tell you that
Thoughts of you
Memories of our time together
Never leave my mind
I can tell you
When I can not communicate with you
I am overtaken by my emotions

Please release me from this time out
I swear I will repent
My horrible past and try… just try…
Please be patient

In your absence…..
Suffering is inevitable
I see no way out….
But in?

# Still entranced by my beloved

The calm after the storm
Is just as exhilarating if not more so
Then the storm itself
I am even more entranced by your aura
Then ever before

New levels of emotions
Intensify life experiences
New levels of trust
Intensify the symbolic embrace I feel
As I gaze into the gateway to your soul

Being nervous can be selfish
we should be honest & truly express to our beloved
that we cannot exist without them
I pray that time will be merciful
to me, To you, To us

I pray that time will find us together
For this life, and our lives yet to be

# True Love

I know I will never be equal to you
I do not want to be
If i were pressed to give a ratio
Between you and me
I would say 49/51

I always want you on top
In every conceivable situation
There is no growth in life
Without pressure
There is not peace in life
Without order and justice

Know safety, know peace
Know order, know serenity
Give up your doubt
Hang onto faith
And find the one true love

# God help me endure

True progress is slow
Torturous to the soul, body & mind
Yet, holds promise for a better tomorrow
For a better future

I pray every day for the strength
To withstand this pressure
I thought the old man died
But apparently, he still has a hold on me

I need to let him go, before I can be free
I need to let him go, before I becomes, "US"
As much as I am pained by this
Mental arrangement with the old man
He has owned me for so long
I am not sure I know how To let Go

# I am truly blessed & anointed

I have always believed in angels
But I have never seen one
Until I have seen you
My love, my soul, my inspiration

I am entranced by your gaze
I feel the hand of God
Hold my beating heart
And tell it
"Be Still, I am here"

I feel the holy spirit
Stir inside of me
I feel the warmth of love
Encompass my authentic self

Honor, Love, Joy and Peace
Reign
Where darkness used to reside
The essence of your being free my soul

I am and shall be eternally beholden

# When I look into my heart....I find you

Every week, I look into your eyes
My soul feels tortured
Every week I look into your eyes
My heart wants to confess all
Of its hidden desires

Yet it is always blocked by fear
For the first time in my life
There is no ulterior motive
I have no destination in mind

The truth is heavy on the Toung
It needs to be set free
In order for the true life to begin
I seek, I wait, I pray for God to

Set my words free

# My soul is free

Under a starry sky
Memories of a time yet to be
I sit under my tree of life
And ponder upon my own existence

Did I exist before I became
Entranced by your existence my beloved
Did I know how to breathe
Before you effectively taught me how

Did I know what the life really was?
Before you entered my personal space
Did I know what love was?
Before your soul became entwined with mine

Time is eternal
Love is fleeting
With or without you here
My heart is engaged
My soul is free

# Thank you

Thank you, my love,
For the comfort I feel within myself
Thank you, my love,
For teaching me the value of silence
The cleansing power of a teardrop

Shame has no place in my love
Shame no longer has a hold over my soul
I intend to travel with your life view for all my days
I intend to sleep every night under a peaceful orange moon
That I see when think about the entrance way to your soul

My mind is alert, My heart is receptive
Thanks to you my love for my new day
Thank you my reason for existence
For my change of view

Seagulls tell me summer is here
Leaves fall to tell me summer will return
After a short rest
I enjoy the sun......
I also enjoy the moon

# Enjoy the Journey

Sitting in my night-time escape pod
I am dreaming of your symbolic embrace
As I gaze into the portal to your soul
That usually ends up
In the deepest part of my heart, mind, and soul

I am still entranced my beloved
I am still in anticipation of our every meeting
Time exists and does not exist
When our paths do not cross in any way

I envision you all day
And I fantasize you are with me
All hours of the night
The night is the hottest part of the day
When I envision you near

Keep me in anticipation
I will enjoy this time
I know the wait time
Will only make the destination sweeter

In any case, I never want to reach the destination
I am enjoying this journey with you

# True Love Ways

My beloved, I depend on you to free me
My heart, my mind, my soul
Oh, my love, when you are near
All reality fades, and I feel left alone
With my dreams of untold desires

I need you to show me the path
To your true love ways
I need you to cool me down
When I become lost in my passions

My only requirement in this life
Is the ability to experience your existence
In any manner within my reach

My soul sours with the eagles
When you are in proximity to me
My heart feels euphoria
When I feel your essence near

# How can I say what I do not know?

How can I say that I love you?
These words do not do justice to the
Complexity of emotions that arise
When you are in proximity to me

I am in deep admiration
The sky opens and I am entranced
As my soul enters into the fifth dimension
In this dimension there is no anxiety, no fear
No lack of trust
All live-in harmony, all live in love
All are free to exist in a world
Free of inequity

# A prayer for Solace

This week I refrained from emailing you
I realized/ I am realizing how I feel
You consume my mind, my heart, my soul
At all times of the day & night
You are my first thought in the morning
My last thought at night

I was praying for this mental distance to help me forget
I was praying for this emotional distance to clear my head
To no avail; my emotions run deeper
My soul rises higher
In addition, I miss you like the flower misses the sun
During the thunderstorm of life

God, I beg you for solace
I pray that time ends my personal affliction
Of my own making
Due to the fact that I remain uncommunicative
To my love regarding my genuine amorous emotions

# I pray for emancipation

Oh my, my, my, my beloved
You know what I want, you know what I need
Do I need to ask you for it? Beg you for it?
I do not want to seem distressed
But I am, I am so very anguished
To the very abyss of my soul

What I need runs deep and is strong, mighty and resilient
I can only receive this from you my beloved
You are in my heart, mind, and soul
Please free me so my mind can be once again at ease

The suppression of my emotions is endangering my life force
I desire for you to penetrate my soul
For you to emancipate my heart
To understand why it is taking so long

To declare my most intimate emotions
In your companionship
The only solace that I have are these words
I am writing and
The small pray I send to God every day and night
To untie my Tongue

And to be able to express my unbridled emotions
To you and only you, my Beloved

# My Auspicious day has finally arrived

My heart is engaged
My soul has been penetrated
My mind is attempting to
Discover how this has happened

I am separated from my past
Yet not quite to my destiny
I search, I seek, I try to find refuge
Within my version of reality

Thoughts of my beloved are what drive me
To continue down this path
Thoughts of his auspicious nature
Motivate me to be my best self

I have never been so lost
Yet found simultaneously
My mind is free, my heart is on fire

My soul regulates me

# Find me, Free me, Embrace me

My love, My beloved
When I look into your eyes I see
A reflection of what I want reality to be
And I know that I can trust you

My love
I need to feel you deep inside me
For my heart, mind & soul to find it's center
To find tranquility in my existence

I know all I need to know concerning my love
I know I can find peace & tranquility when you are near
I know you will never let me drown in my desires
I know you will always save me from my own irrationality
And deliver me to the promise land where I can feel

Warm flowing waters
Dreams that inspire growth
Desires that inspire greatness
Every day brings me closer to the day
I can feel you inside me once again

When you are near, I can embrace my true nature
Without fear
I can embrace new and exciting outlets

That were unknown to me before
I found my heart's greatest desire

The torture of missing you
Is far less than
The thought of
Living without you

When I can feel you deep inside me
I feel strong, I feel who I am on the inside
Ooh, deeper
I can feel it,
I can feel intense eternal euphoria

When I look into your eyes
I see who I want to be
I feel emancipation knocking
At my heart's door

The hesitation to answer is strong
Avoidance has been programmed since before my birth
my soul yearns to be free
To swim in the unfulfilled desires
Of my heart

You represent what I most desire
Thank you for protecting me
Thank you for hypnotizing me
I speak about the magic in your eyes
That makes me forget about all the world
Except for my heart's one sincere desire

www.ingramcontent.com/pod-product-compliance
Lightning Source LLC
Chambersburg PA
CBHW061328120626
46546CB00007B/2722